YOU ARE FREAKING AWESOME!

FREE YOURSELF FROM STRESS AND ANXIETY WITH DAILY AFFIRMATIONS
AND INSPIRATIONAL QUOTES

PICK ME READ ME PRESS

ISBN 979-888606501-5

YOU ARE FREAKING FABULOUS!

- Keep your head up.
- Be proud of yourself.
- Take your time.

THIS BOOK BELONGS TO:

____

BY PICK ME READ ME PRESS

Contents

Contents

I am gratefull for all that I have

I AM
GRATEFUL
FOR ALL
THAT I HAVE

Believe you can and you're half way there.

Believe you can
and you're
halfway there.

Trust the timing of your life.

TRUST
the timing
of your Life

I am brave, bold and beautiful!

I AM BRAVE, BOLD
and beautiful

Enter Caption

My imperfections make me unique.

My imperfections
make me
unique.

I believe in myself.

I BELIEVE
IN
MYSELF

I will not worry about things I cannot control.

I will
not worry
about things
I CANNOT
control

My confidence knows no limits.

MY CONFIDENCE KNOWS NO LIMITS.

I am bold, beautiful and brilliant.

I AM BOLD
Beautiful
and brilliant.

Everything will work out for me.

Everything
will
work out
for me

I am free to create the life I desire.

I AM FREE
TO CREATE
THE LIFE
I DESIRE

I can absolutely do anything I put my mind to.

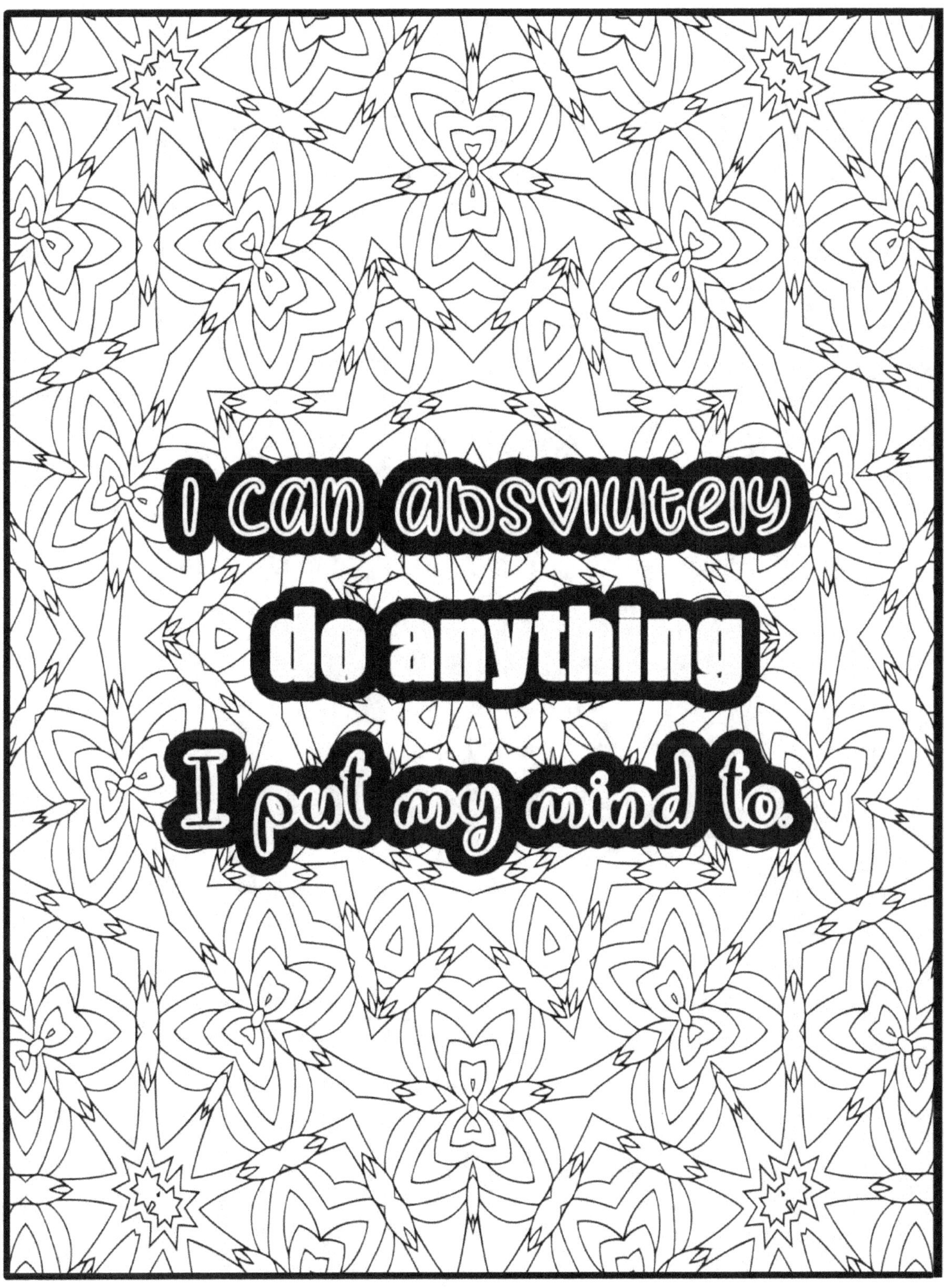
I can absolutely
do anything
I put my mind to.

Every day, in every way, I am becoming better and better.

CHAPTER FOURTEEN

I grow and become a better version of myself every day.

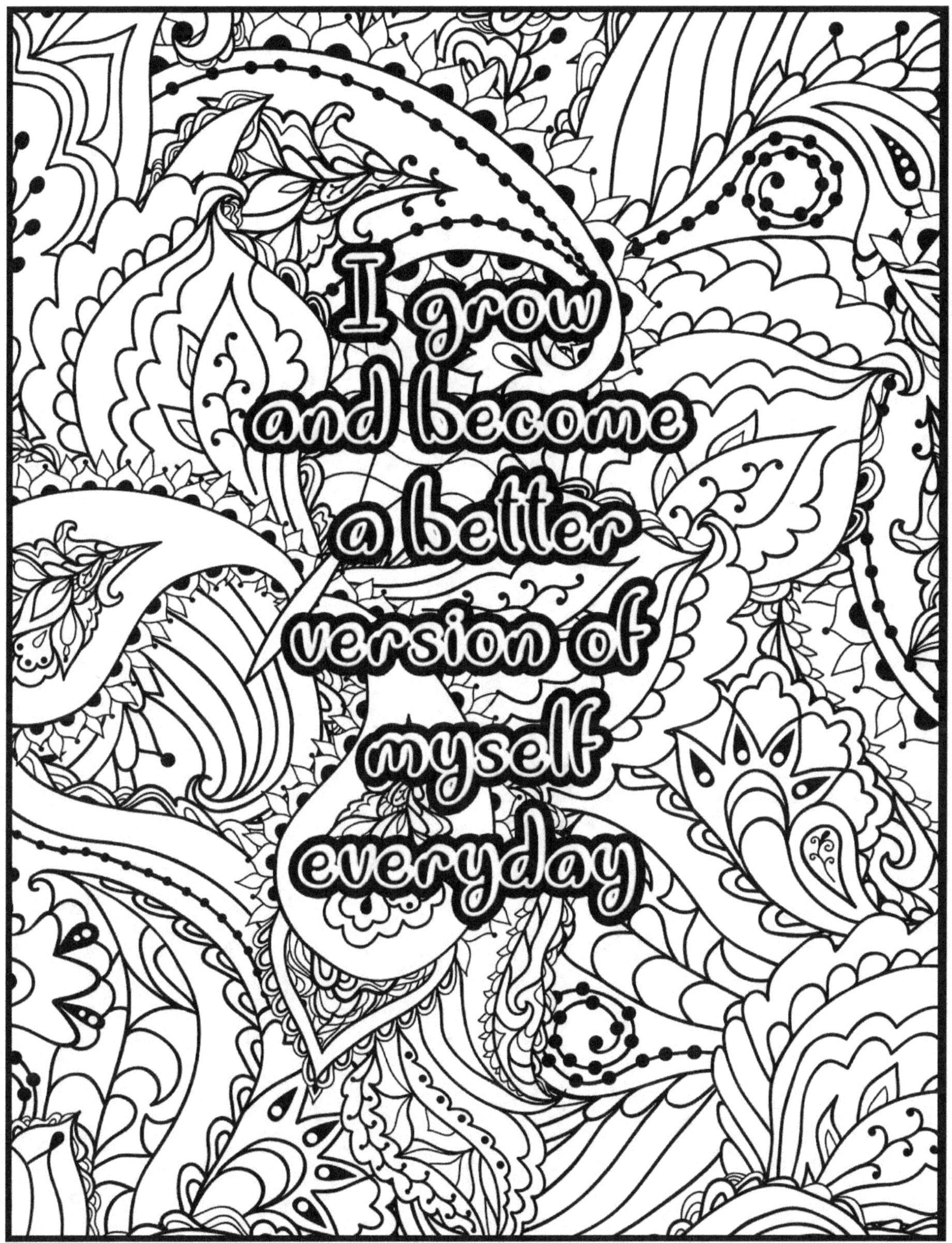

Enter Caption

Learn from yesterday, live for today, hope for tomorrow.

Learn from yesterday,
live for today,
hope for tomorrow.

CHAPTER SIXTEEN

It's OK if I make mistakes.

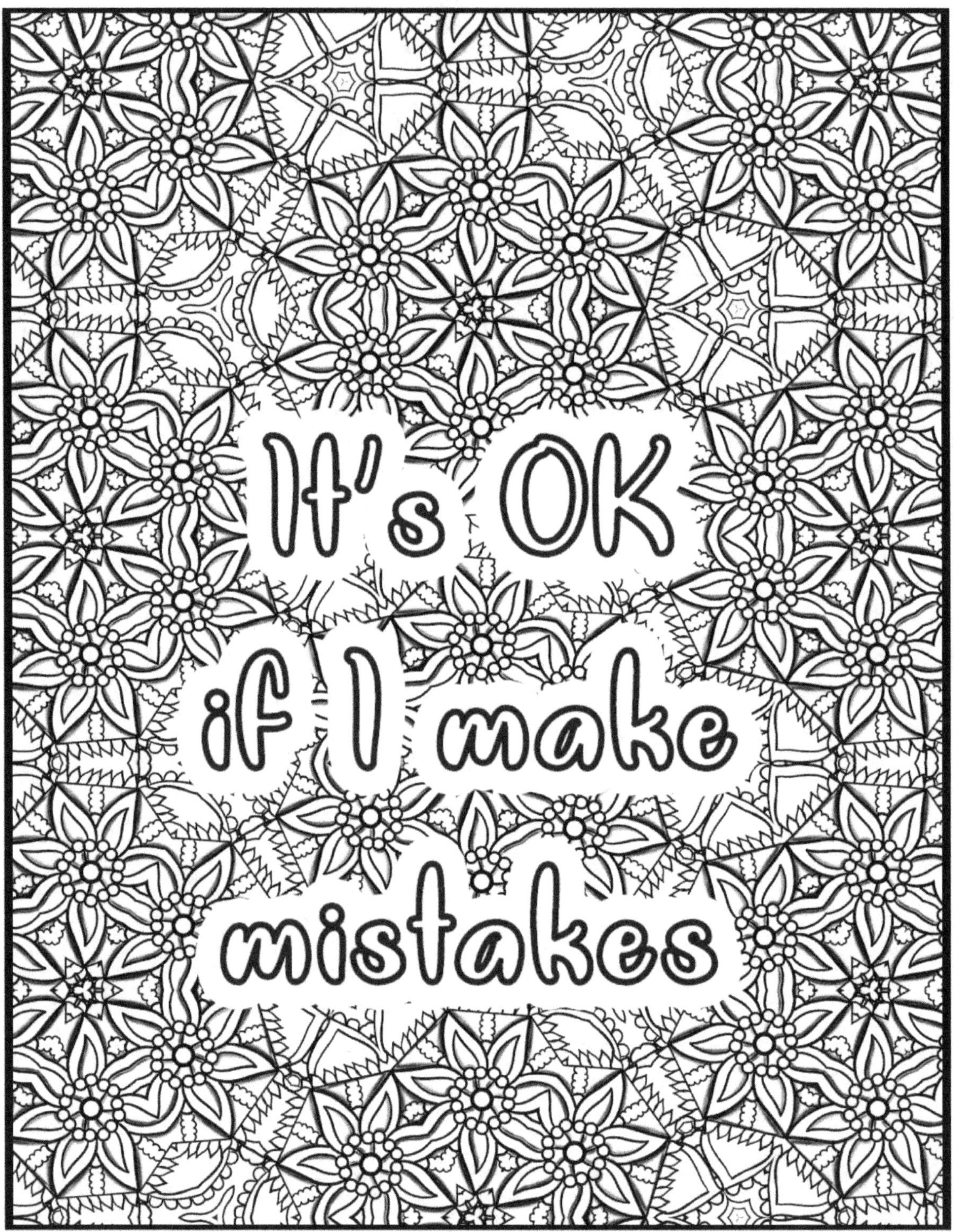

Enter Caption

I chose to stay positive and never give up.

Enter Caption

I am enough.

Enter Caption

• 41 •

My past is not a reflection of my future.

My past
is not
a reflection
of my future.

Everything I need is within me.

Enter Caption

I live in an abundant life, in an abundant universe.

I live in an
ABUNDANT Life
in an abundant
universe

I choose peace.

I CHOOSE
PEACE

I deserve to have joy in my life.

I deserve
to have JOY
in my Life

I forgive so that I can feel better.

I forgive
so that
I can feel
better

I let go of all that no longer serves me.

I let go of all
that no longer
serves me

CHAPTER TWENTY-SIX

I accept myself unconditionally.

I accept myself unconditionally

I am blessed with an amazing family and friends.

I am blessed
with an amazing
family and
friends.

I am doing my best and that is enough.

I am doing
my best
and that is
Enough

My body is healthy & I am grateful.

My body
is Healthy
I am
Grateful

Your limitation is only your imagination.

YOUR LIMITATION
ITS ONLY
YOUR IMAGINATION

I choose hope over fear.

CHAPTER THIRTY-ONE

I choose
HOPE
over
FEAR

Never give up because great things take time.

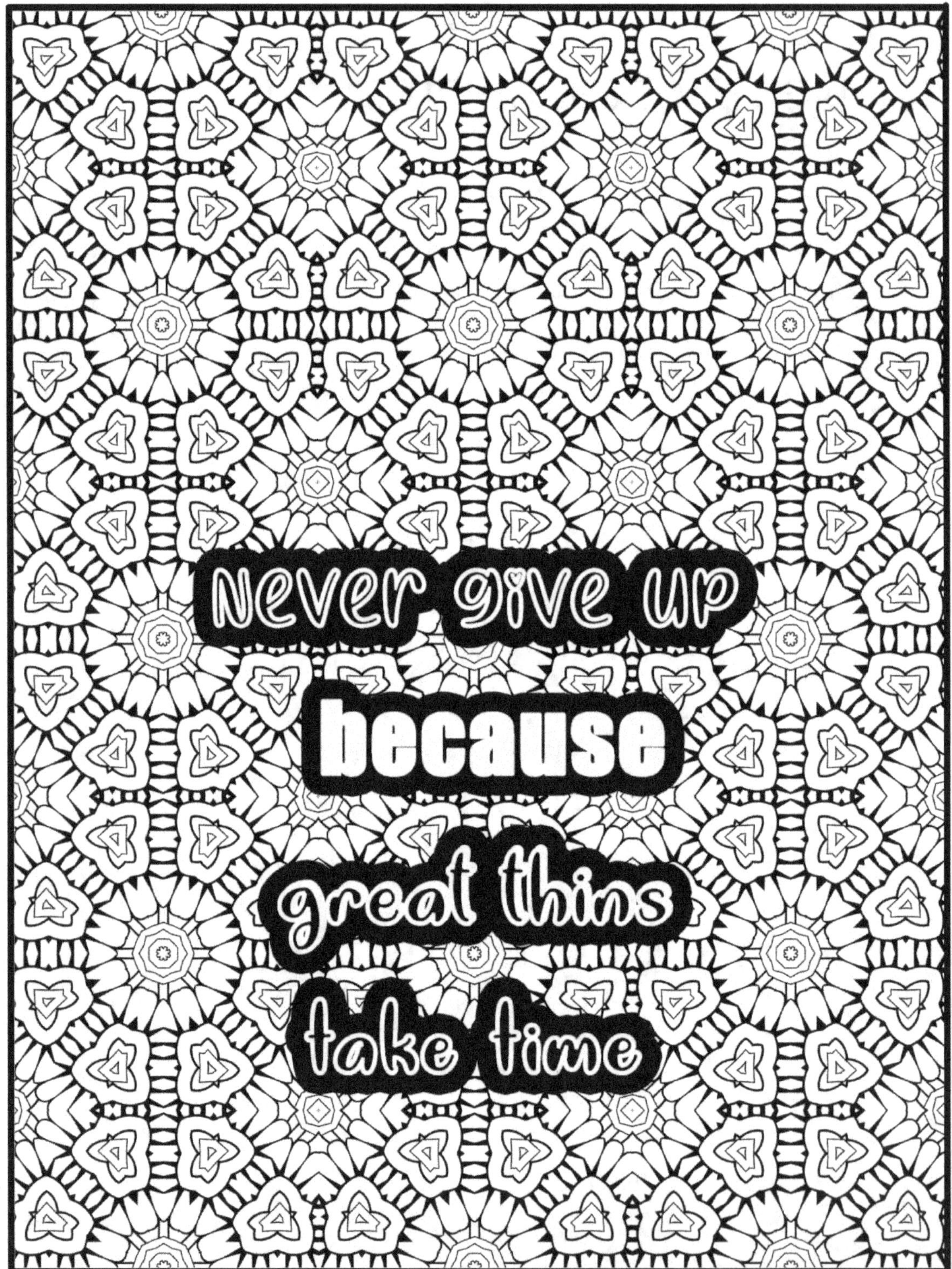

Enter Caption

Today I choose joy.

Today
I CHOOSE
JOY

The best is yet to come.

THE BEST
IS YET
TO COME

There is no elevation to success. You have to take the stairs.

There is no elevation
to success.
You have to
take the stairs.

You are much stronger than you think you are.

CHAPTER THIRTY-SIX

You are
much stronger
than
you think
you are.

I can easily create a life I love.

I can easily
create
a Life
I LOVE

Forget the mistake. Remember the lesson.

Forget the mistake
Remember the
LESSON

I will step out of my comfort zone and try something new today.

Thank You!

Thank you!

We hope you enjoyed our book.

As a small family company, your feedback is very important to us .

Please let us know how you like our book at :

pickme.readme@gmail.com

* 9 7 9 8 8 8 6 0 6 5 0 1 5 *